NORTH AND SOUTH:

OR

FOUR QUESTIONS CONSIDERED:

WHAT HAVE WE DONE? WHAT HAVE WE TO DO?
WHAT HAVE WE TO HOPE? WHAT HAVE WE TO FEAR?

A SERMON

PREACHED IN THE FIRST CHURCH IN HARTFORD,

ON THE

DAY OF THE NATIONAL FAST, SEPT. 26TH, 1861.

By J. HAWES, D. D.

HARTFORD:
PRESS OF CASE, LOCKWOOD AND COMPANY.
1861.

HARTFORD, Sept. 28, 1861.

Rev. J. HAWES, D. D.

Dear Sir:—We, the subscribers, having heard the discourse delivered by you on the day of the National Fast, are desirous to see it in print, for our own benefit as well as for the interest of those who were not present at its delivery. We therefore request a copy for publication.

Yours Very Respectfully,

W. W. ELLSWORTH,
JAMES B. HOSMER,
STEPHEN SPENCER,
WM. W. TURNER,
OLCOTT ALLEN,
JOHN BEACH,
S. S. CHAMBERLIN,
TH. S. WILLIAMS,
SAMUEL S. WARD,
LEONARD CHURCH,
THOMAS SMITH,
H. A. PERKINS,
JAS. G. BATTERSON,
ALBERT DAY,
A. M. SMITH,
WARREN G. JONES,
Rev. S. B. PAGE, Cleveland, O.
CALVIN DAY,
H. BLANCHARD,
S. M. CAPRON,
D. F. ROBINSON.

HARTFORD, Sept. 30, 1861.

Hon. W. W. Ellsworth and others:

GENTLEMEN:—The discourse you request for publication, I readily commit to your disposal, in the hope that it may do good.

Yours Respectfully,

J. HAWES.

SERMON.

I NEVER expected to see a time like this, when every day, and at all times of the day, we see soldiers in arms and hear the sound of martial exercises along our streets, and about the avenues of our city. I never expected to be called to preach on an occasion like the present,—a day of humiliation, fasting and prayer, appointed by the President of the United States, in conformity with the recommendation of both houses of Congress, and seconded by the chief magistrate of our own State,—on account of war, civil war having broke out in our country, and which is spreading devastation and ruin over the land. I never rose to address an audience, when I was so much at a loss what to say, in order to meet the demands of the occasion, and at the same time not to offend against the dignity and sacredness of my office as a minister of Christ. As I look round on this assembly, and think of the circumstances in which we meet here to day, a solemn awe comes over my mind, and I tremble lest I shall prove unfaithful to my trust, or fail to meet the reasonable expectations of those whom I address. May God guide the service and make it profitable to us all.

I find a text suited to my purpose, in 1 Sam., 17 ; 29:—AND DAVID SAID,—WHAT HAVE I NOW DONE? IS THERE NOT A CAUSE?

The case was this :—

The Philistines, whose country bordered on the south and west of Judea, made war upon the people of Israel, and gathered their armies at Schochoh, which belonged to Judah. Saul and the men of Israel gathered together their hosts and pitched by the valley of Elah, over against the Philistines. On this occasion an aged Israelite who had eight sons, sent three of them into the army, while David the youngest was retained at home to keep his father's sheep at Bethlehem. The father, naturally anxious for the three sons in the army, sent David with provisions for them, and bade him inquire how his brethren fared, and to take their pledge. Leaving the sheep with a keeper, David rose up early in the morning, and hastened to execute his mission of sympathy and kindness. He reached the camp as the host was going forth to fight, and ran into the army and saluted his brethren. Here it was that he contemplated the approaching storm, which threatened to overwhelm his country. Here he saw the battle in array with fierce invaders, led on by a champion, whose stature and prowess were only equalled by his pride and blasphemy. He heard no terms proposed but absolute submission and slavery. The whole bearing and look, and defiant menace of the proud man, Goliath of Gath, were appalling, and Israel fled at his presence as he marched forth at the head of armed hosts, bidding defiance to the hosts of Israel. A holy indignation rose in the bosom of the young shepherd, and he panted to enter into the conflict that he might take away the reproach from his countrymen, and show that there was courage which was ready to meet the challenge of the champion, with all his pride and impious boasting. But what could he do? He was there as a private man, and not as a soldier. Yet he could not restrain the flame that glowed within and impelled him to the battle. So he modestly inquired, what shall be done to the man that killeth this Philistine and taketh away the reproach from Israel? For who is this uncircumcised Philistine, that he should defy the armies of the living God. Eliab his eldest brother, heard when he spake thus, and his anger was enkindled against him; and he said,—why camest thou down hither? and with whom hast thou left those few sheep in the wilderness? I know thy pride, and the naughtiness of thy heart, for thou art come down that thou mightest see the battle. And David said,—what have I now done? Is there not a cause? As if he had said—have I done anything wrong, or anything which I had not a just cause for doing? Came I not down at the command of my father? Is it not right that I should feel indignation at the blasphemies and boastings which I have heard, and should have an earnest desire to bear a part in withstanding the enemies of my country and of my God, in their impiety and rage? The reply of David was just. It proceeded from a true love of his country, and showed a willingness to do what he could to repel the foe then encamped on its borders and warring for its overthrow.

The text suggests my subject and in pursuing it, I shall attempt an answer to four questions.—

What have we done; what have we to do; what have we to hope; and what have we to fear. Let us consider,

1. What have we done? I mean we at the North; we in the free States; what have we done to provoke the wrath of the South and bring on the terrible war which has burst upon us, like thunder from a clear sky? But a few months since, we were a united and happy people. All the great interests of the country were in a high state of prosperity, and the prospect of a long bright future in reserve for us was perhaps never more promising. Now we are a divided people, the union is rent asunder; fourteen of the States have rushed away from the constitution, and having formed themselves into a confederacy, are carrying on a war against the remaining States, and threatening the overthrow of our government. Terrible guilt attaches to one party or the other, engaged in this conflict. To which does it belong, to the

North, or the South; to the slave States or the free. I have long and earnestly sought to know the truth on this subject; to discover what articles of indictment the South could bring against us to justify the course she has seen fit to adopt in this unnatural and terrible conflict. And I must confess that after the most careful inquiry, I have been unable to discover any one cause for the war that can for a moment stand the test of truth or sound reason; and I am constrained still to ask, what have we done? We have violated no principle of the constitution; we have resisted no law of Congress; we have invaded none of the rights of the South; we have despoiled none of her citizens of their property; we have done violence to none of them while visiting at the North or residing among us on business; we have driven none of them from our midst as exiles; we have tarred and feathered none of them, and we have seized and put to death none of them in violation of all forms of law, and with no charge of crime, but that of thinking and speaking as free men and christians. We stand clear of each and of all these offenses; and I know not that they have been alleged against us by any southern man of competent knowledge and candor to judge in the case. But all these offenses, these outrages, it is well known, have been repeatedly committed against us by and at the South, and under circumstances of peculiar and irritating aggravation. And yet we have peaceably and patiently borne all; have borne insults and provocations, and wrongs inflicted upon our worthy citizens, which, if inflicted by any foreign power, would have been deemed a just cause of war. What then have we done? Have we passed personal liberty bills? That is true. But they were not designed to nullify or violate any law of Congress, or to prevent the reclamation of any slave who could be legally proved to have escaped from his master; and I have seen it stated on good authority, that no master ever did fail of regaining his fugitive slave through the operation of these terrible liberty bills of which so much has been said. These bills were enacted, some of them many years ago, as a safe-guard to our own colored people, to prevent their being kidnapped, and carried off to be sold in a southern market; and they have all, I believe, so far as they have any bearing on the matter in controversy, been repealed.

Is it alleged that we have agitated the subject of slavery; have insisted on the right of discussing it from the pulpit and the press, and of exposing its wrongs and its villainies? That is true; but is the insisting on this right a just cause for treason and war? or is it a right to be abandoned by free men at the dictation of the slave power? Is it alleged, again, that we have refused to allow to slavery a right to extend itself over all and every part of our free territory, and have insisted that it should be confined, henceforth, within its own legal and constitutional boundaries? That, also, is true. But what wrong is done to the South by this? We claim no right over slavery in the States where it now exists by local or State laws, and we have no wish to invade the laws or resist the authority which are spread over it on its own soil. But when the claim is set up that it has a right to travel side by side with freedom, and to establish itself wherever free territory is to be found in our whole domain, we resist the claim as unjust and wicked; we say it has no foundation in the constitution, nor in the known sentiments of the framers of that instrument, nor in the law of nature, and certainly not in the law of God and the principles of His gospel. Standing on this ground, we say of slavery, lifting up its imperious voice and demanding more territory and a wider domain over which to spread its misery and its crimes,—hitherto thou mayest come, but no further; and here thy proud waves shall be stayed. And is not this right?

Is it alleged, again, that we have attempted to wield the powers of the Federal government to the prejudice of the South? But wherein have we done this? The powers of the government have been essentially in the hands of the South for the last thirty years, and scarcely a demand has she made since the beginning of our government, relating to her peculiar institution, which has not been conceded by the North.* At the formation of the constitution, she insisted that the slave-trade should be continued twenty years, and it was allowed; she insisted that three-fifths of her slaves should be added to her free population as represented in Congress, and that protection, to a certain extent, should be extended over this species of live stock, and all this was conceded to her. In 1793, she wanted a fugitive slave law passed, and Congress passed such a law. In 1820, she wanted the Missouri Compromise, and it was given her. In 1854, she wanted the Missouri Compromise repealed, and it was done. She next asked for a judicial decision of the territorial question in her favor, and the Supreme Court of the United States, in contravention of the whole current of our legislation, so decided. State after State, I know not how many, have been brought into the Union with the mark and the curse of slavery upon them, to satisfy her demands; and I find it stated, on competent authority, that in various ways, to promote the interests of the very States now leading this rebellion, the people of the United States, acting through Congress, have paid over $617,000,000.† Indeed, I do not recollect more than one instance, that of Kansas, in which the South has failed to obtain the concessions from government in favor of slavery which she asked for. And for all these concessions we now have the miserable return of an organized rebellion and a

* See Everett's Oration, p. 38.

† Senator Latham's speech, July 20, 1861.

wicked attempt to break up the government. Nothing, in fact, could satisfy the South. Her demands became more and more imperious and unreasonable, till it was found that they must be resisted or the whole country come under the rule of an unprincipled slave oligarchy. The question then returns,—What have we done? Nothing, surely, to provoke this horrible fratricidal war, nor to hasten it on. We conceded and compromised; we bore and forebore till the country was pushed to the very brink of ruin. And it is my full belief, that had the government remained in the hands of the South another four years, the day of redemption would have been passed and our subjection to the slave power would have been inevitable. The people saw this—the free people of the North and West, and roused by a sense of danger, they united and in a perfectly constitutional way elected a president of their own principles, and of course to the disapprobation and dislike of the South. This tells the whole story. The free North have chosen a man to administer the government for the next four years, in the spirit and on the principles on which it was founded by our fathers. This is the whole head and front of our offending. Hence the war. No act of injustice, oppression or wrong on our part can be pleaded by the South in justification of her secession and rebellion. Long before Mr. Lincoln was inaugurated, or a single act had been done by him or the incoming administration, the whole plan of secession was matured and the fatal blow ready to be struck; the signal was given; war was commenced; State after State rushed out of the Union and joined in a conspiracy, a rebellion against constitutional authority. The programme, formed long before, was carried out in mad haste; a new government was formed; forts, arsenals, navy yards, ships, mints, and all kinds of United States property lying within the seceding States were seized and used to strengthen and carry on the rebellion, till at length the nation's flag was smitten down and trailed in the dust, and the cry went up throughout the South,—On to Washington, take possession of the capital and the victory is ours. Up to this point our government waited patiently,—waited too long, as we all now feel, but waited in hope that the madness which ruled the hour would subside, and reason once more resume its sway. But when all hope of pacification by forbearance and patient waiting passed away, and it was seen that rebellion must be put down by the strong arm of power, or destroy the country, there was witnessed the uprising of a mighty people, rushing to arms at the call of the President, gathering around our capital and along the borders of the rebel states, ready to shed their blood and sacrifice their all to defend their country and maintain its government and its laws.

So the case stands to day. An army of from two hundred and fifty to three hundred thousand men, stationed in different sections of the country, ready to be set in battle array against, perhaps an equal number from the seceding States; the scene is grand; it is awful; the end is not yet; the future is veiled from our sight; we must wait the issue, trusting in that God who rules in righteousness over all.

II. We pass to our second question. What have we to do? What does duty, right, demand of us, in the circumstances in which our country, and we as individuals, are placed? And,—

1. We must have a right understanding, of the nature, cause and object of the conflict now going on in the country. As to its nature, it is not properly speaking, a war. War is a struggle between two sovereign nations appealing to arms for the settlement of their difficulties. But the South is not a sovereign nation, not acknowledged to be such by a single

government on earth. They are a conspiracy; a treasonable banding together of a portion of the one nation of the United States to break up the Union, and destroy the government. The whole plan, in its inception, development and progress, is properly characterized as a rebellion, a wicked insurrection against constitutional authority; and the effort now being made by loyal men to put it down, by force of arms, is not, I repeat, in any proper sense, war, any more than it is war when a city police puts forth its power to quell a riot or a mob, or to defend innocent citizens against the assaults of thieves and robbers. The most scrupulous advocate of peace might go into this contest without violating one of his peace principles, just as he might defend himself or his family against a house breaker or a murderer. It is not war when criminals are seized and punished, or when pirates aud traitors are put down and brought to justice by an armed force. It is simply an act of self defense, a vindication of right by the punishment of crime. So the contest that is now going on in this country, it is simply a struggle for self defense; a putting forth of the armed power of the country to defend its nationality, to maintain its existence indeed, against rebels combined for its overthrow.

As to the right of secession as claimed by the South, it has not the shadow of a reason for its support. Secession! Secession from the Republic; secession from the one constitution, binding the Republic together as one nation, one people, and one for all time. Secession is an absurdity wholly opposed to the spirit and form of our government, contrary to the known sentiments of the fathers of the republic, the great statesmen who framed the constitution and enacted the fundamental laws of the nation, and it seems never to have been thought of as a possibility, till it was hatched in the brain of Mr. Calhoun, of South Carolina, and since taken up and propagated by uneasy, ambitious, reckless spirits at the South.

With regard to the cause of this gigantic rebellion, I have before said, that its immediate cause was the election of Mr. Lincoln to the presidency. The whole spirit and policy of the South, in entering on the late presidential election, meant this,—"If we can succeed in electing our candidate, as we have in fifteen that have preceded it, well and good; but if we fail, we intend to prostrate the government and break up the Union; peaceably if we can, otherwise at the point of the sword."* They failed, and immediately they set themselves to carry out their predetermined purpose. They rushed like madmen for the destruction of the Union, just because they were defeated in the election and were made to feel that the power of the government, which they had wielded for so long a period, essentially for sixty years, had passed out of their hands, not probably to return again. This was more than southern chivalry could bear. So the appeal was made to arms, and we have been constrained to meet them on that ground.

And what is the object we aim at in the position we have taken? It is not conquest; it is not subjugation; it is not to spread carnage and bloodshed over the States in revolt; but only to stay the hand of violence, they have raised against us; to bring them back to their allegiance and maintain the government of the country, which they have wickedly conspired to overthrow, and thus preserve the constitution and the laws, which we and they have alike sworn to support.

Is it said that the object of the war is to destroy slavery, by setting free the four millions of human beings now held in bondage at the South? I deny that this was or is the object of the war; though I can not but pray earnestly, as I confidently hope, that in the good providence of God, the overthrow of slavery will be the consequence, the ultimate result of the

* Everett's N. York Oration, July 4, 1861.

conflict. But this was not, nor is it now, its avowed or its real object. That is to maintain our government; to defend our Republican institutions; to put down rebellion and restore the country, the *whole country*, to the state of peace, prosperity and strength which it has so long enjoyed, to the wonder and admiration of the nations. This is the sole object for which we send forth our armies, pour out our treasures and sacrifice our sons and our brethren on the bloody field. And this object is worth all that it will or can cost us. The war in which we are engaged is not for ourselves alone, or our posterity; but for the world and for all time. The question of the possibility of maintaining free institutions is now on trial before the nations; the problem of free government is now to be settled; and if we fail, if the grand experiment inaugurated by our fathers and so long and so successfully carried forward in our hands, shall now fail, and our country sink into a state of anarchy, or be divided into separate sovereign States, contiguous, jealous, ever exposed to make war on each other,—I for one should feel that the sun of freedom had gone back on the dial of time for generations and for centuries, and might never rise again. It was said by a great French statesman, M. Fould, to an American citizen not long ago, after the rebellion broke out,—"Your Republic is dead. And it is probably the last the world will ever see. You will have a reign of terrorism, and after that two or three monarchies." All this is likely to be verified if this revolution succeed.

This then is one thing we have to do,—to understand well the nature, the cause and the object of the contest in which we are engaged and the momentous interests involved in the issue.

2. Another thing we have to do is to strive for a union of all parties. This is not a time to carry out our personal pref-

erences, or to stick to and maintain our party attachments. It is a time which calls for the union of all true men in the one great issue which is now pending before the country. Let there be none to contend for old party lines, and none to attempt to form new parties, and, least of all, to cry peace, compromise, adjustment, while the roar of cannon is in our ears, or the sword at our breasts. Lord Nelson caused to be signaled from the topmast of his ship, just as he was going into the battle of Trafalgar, these memorable words,—" England expects every man to do his duty." A like signal I seem to see inscribed on our country's flag, in this time of her peril, America expects every citizen to do his duty. It has been well said, by a true statesman,—' We may differ as to many things in the past; we may differ as to many things in the future; but we must now act for the present. And for the present there is but one course for us all to pursue. Our misguided brethren at the South have left us no alternative but to fight. Our capital must be defended; our flag must be sustained. The authority of the government must be vindicated. The great experiment must be fully and fairly tried of restoring the Union upon its old constitutional basis.' And whatever is necessary for the accomplishment of these ends must be promptly and thoroughly done. Let there be, then, no hanging back; no drawing off into little squads or parties; no secret counsels and plots devised in conclave to embarrass our government or lead any to withhold from it their hearty co-operation and support.

In the last speech made by Mr. Douglas to his party at Chicago, but a short time before his death, he uttered these memorable words: " Whoever is not prepared to sacrifice party organizations and platforms on the altar of his country, does not deserve the support of honest people. We must cease discussing party issues, make no allusion to old party tests, have no criminations or recriminations, indulge in no taunts one against another as to what has been the cause of these troubles." This is sound advice and should be followed by all, of every political party.

After what has now been said, it is scarcely necessary to add, that another thing we have to do is, to stand by the constitution and maintain our government and our nationality at all hazards. That sacred instrument, the bond of our Union and the basis of our prosperity and happiness, cost our fathers too much blood and treasure to be surrendered, without a struggle, to the hand of violence now raised to destroy it. And our government, based on the constitution, and our nationality, growing out of it,—they must be defended whatever it may cost. Our very life as a nation depends on this. It is no time to talk of peace, of concession, compromise, re-adjustment, while rebellion maintains its posture of defiance and insists upon having what it demands, or fighting us unto the death. Peace is a charming word; I love the very sound of it; and the blessings it carries in its bosom are inestimable. But peace sought and obtained by cowing down to the South and conceding to her demands would be infinite dishonor; it could result, at the best, only in a temporary suspension of hostilities, shortly to break out again in a spirit of violence and hate greater than ever. No; let the question be settled now, and settled for all time, whether our constitution and government shall stand and we remain a free nation, or whether we shall sink into anarchy and confusion, to be adjusted in the end by the reign of despotism, or some other reign of oppression and wrong, like that which enters into the new Confederacy of the South, which, according to the declaration of its Vice-President, Mr. Stephens, rests on slavery as its corner stone, on the great truth, as he calls it, that the inferior is to be held in subordination to the superior race.

Shall we succumb to a power like this,—a power that bases itself on slavery as its chief foundation, and whose great aim is to perpetuate and extend the system as widely as possible? No, never, never. Let us, then, one and all, without distinction of party, gather around the citadel of our constitution and our free forms of government, and resolve that, come weal or woe, we will in life and in death, now and forever, stand up and defend them *with our lives, our fortunes, and our sacred honor.*

Another thing we have to do, and that is freely and manfully to meet and bear the burdens that may come upon us in carrying this conflict through to a triumphant issue. The cost *will* be, it *has* already been great, but not too great for the object to be attained. It cost our fathers seven years of war to achieve our independence and establish the government which we are now called to defend; and the burdens which they cheerfully and magnanimously bore in that long and bloody conflict were greater, far, far greater, compared with their number and their ability, than can be expected to come upon us, even should the present war last twice seven years. The men and the resources of the free States are abundant to meet every exigency that can reasonably be expected to arise. Our late war with Mexico cost us 217,175,575 dollars; but this sum, vast as it appears, was paid with no perceptible inconvenience or pressure upon the people at large. So it will be with the present war. It will for a time embarrass business and depress commerce and trade; and the usual sources of income enjoyed by many will be diminished or perhaps entirely cut off. What then? Why, there will be a necessity for curtailment of personal and family expenses and the practice of self-denial and greater economy and industry, it may be; and something of this kind, far from injuring, might prove a great blessing to many in our land. But come what may, in this or any other form, there should be no shrinking from the expenses necessary to carry on the war; no grumbling on account of taxes, or the accumulation of national debt. Where all is at stake, as in the present case, we may well spare a part of what we have for the sake of saving the rest. It is not we alone who are to suffer if we fail; but our children and our children's children to the latest posterity, and the cause of liberty and free government throughout the world. And then, when peace is restored on right and honorable principles, prosperity will quickly return and new enterprise and thrift spring up on every side, and all departments of business will be waked into new life and be crowned with new success.

Yet another thing we have to do, more important than any or than all that I have yet mentioned, and that is, we have to recognize our relations to God as the great Ruler of the world; to feel our dependence on him for success in this necessary, but terrible conflict; and humbly confessing our sins and the sins of the nation against him, our rightful Lord and Sovereign, to implore the interposition of his gracious power in our behalf, that right may prevail and peace and order and happiness be speedily restored to our divided, warring and bleeding country.

On the duty here indicated, all-important as it is, I have no time to enlarge. There can be no doubt that the fearful judgment that has come upon us as a nation is for our sins. They have risen up to heaven and have long cried for the displeasure of the Most High to be poured down upon us. I need not attempt to particularize. Our great sin as a nation has been forgetfulness of God, disregard of his authority, contempt of his laws, pride, boasting of our strength and our greatness, and setting up for independence of him as the great Ruler and Judge of the world. *Ungodliness*, casting off the fear of Jehovah, ignoring his supremacy, and practically setting aside his right to reign over us,—these are sins that lie with fearful weight upon us as a people, and they are properly the source of the terrible crimes, and frauds, and vices and oppressions, and villanies and wrongs which have, especially of late years, so rapidly increased and spread in all parts of the land. When I think of these things and remember that God is just, I have great misgiving as to the scenes that are opening upon us. The Lord has a controversy with us. His voice crieth in the land, and it becomes us to hear the rod and him who hath appointed it. There is a God. O that our nation knew it,—there is a God of holiness, justice and truth, who ruleth over the world, and the nation and the people that will not obey him he will utterly destroy. Let us not rely too confidently on our superior numbers, nor on our vast resources of money and means, and our indomitable energy and prowess. All these will avail us little if the Lord be risen against us or has come forth for the punishment of our sins. He reigns in righteousness over nations as over men, and if they will not see his hand nor hear his voice when he comes forth kindly to warn and admonish them, he will speak in louder tones and stretch forth a more fearful arm for their punishment, and it may be for their destruction. The signs of the times are dark and ominous. The country is in a perilous condition. She is like a ship in a stormy sea, enveloped in dense fog, with rocks and shoals around her, and no pilot on board who knows the way of escape or how to bring her safely into port. She may escape unharmed, or she may be broken in pieces and become a wreck, amid the storms and waves that are fiercely beating around her. Man sees not the issue. Man has no wisdom and no power adequate to the exigencies of a time like this. God only can still the raging of the sea in its angry upheavings and bring the deliverance we need, and to him it becomes us all to lift up our voice of prayer, and cry in true sincerity and earnestness of spirit,—spare thy people, O Lord, and give not thy heritage to reproach.

Having thus spoken of what we have done, and of what we have to do, I pass next to speak of what we have to hope. And here, looking at the horoscope of time, and scanning, as best I can, the future, hope, I am happy to say, hope is very greatly in the ascendant. True, we know little of what is before us. The book of providence is to us a sealed book, and time is its only interpreter. Still there are signs of the times which we do well to consider, and certain great fixed principles in the divine government by the aid of which we may study the scene now passing in our country, and from them we can not fail, I think, to gather hope, bright hope, for our country's future.

Let me just dot a few particulars which have much weight in my own mind. And,

1. We have much to hope from the goodness of the cause in which we are engaged. That is not for aggression, for conquest, for blood; but for the maintenance of our free government, the best that ever the world saw; for the defense of liberty and righteous law and the suppression of treason and rebellion. If ever there was a good cause, a righteous cause, summoning to its support the best energies of men, that is one which has called for the uprising of a mighty people in our land, and sent them forth by hundreds of thousands to rally under our country's banner and defend it against the wicked assaults of those who have banded together to smite it to the ground. The conflict, as I have before said, is not one of our seeking, nor one of our provoking; it has been forced upon us by the bad counsels and wicked measures of a set of unprincipled, ambitious politi-

cians at the South, misguiding and deceiving the people, and plunging them into a needless, ruinous war. We stand on the defensive. We mean to repel their attacks; to put down the wicked rebellion they have inaugurated, and restore peace and harmony to the country, as soon as it can be done on right principles, and with a due regard to the safety and honor of our government and the prosperity of our free institutions. This, then, is a righteous cause, and as God favors the right, we may gather hope from this, that he will bear us through the contest and crown our arms with victory.

2. We have much to hope from the fact that the civilized world is on our side. What nation on earth has commended the rebellion of the South, or what portion of the christian world has expressed the least sympathy with her in the war she is waging? This war, on her part, is essentially a pro-slavery war. It was undertaken and is carried on for the purpose of extending the domain and perpetuating the institution of slavery. Now slavery is a doomed institution. The whole christian and civilized world are against it; and, standing on the ground we have taken in this war, we also are against it, and are resolved that it shall not go beyond its present prescribed limits; and maintaining this ground, we are sure of the sympathies and good wishes of all the true friends of freedom and religion throughout the world. And if the time should come, when we shall need their aid to bring this conflict to a successful close, that aid, we may rest assured, will not be withheld, but will be forthcoming at our asking.

3. We have much to hope from the remarkable union of the North in sustaining the cause which has forced us on to the battle-field. Was there ever such a sight under heaven as was witnessed when the booming of the cannon that were

fired on Sumpter rolled over the land; the uprising of twenty millions of freemen, ready to repel the assault, and crush the rebellion thus begun? It was a grand, a sublime sight, indicating, it has seemed to me, an impulse, an inspiration from above, waking up the people to a sense of their danger and of their rights, and uniting them in one firm determination to defend them. Parties there were before, and differences of opinion as to matters of policy and the causes of the contest. But the blow struck by the South in the hour of her madness, surprisingly cast these differences into the background, and united all parties with scarcely an exception worthy to be named, into one party, the party for the Union and the government. So essentially it stands to-day throughout the North. The croaking and the whining we hear on this side and that, indicate clearly whence they come, and really the number who make these underground, unpleasant sounds, would seem to be so small as scarcely to be worth naming in the face of the one great united party who are resolved to stand by the Constitution and defend the country in this time of its peril. This augurs well, and gives us good ground to hope for the future.

4. We have much to hope from the Union sentiment which exists at the South. It has been said by one who has the best means of knowing—Senator Holt, of Kentucky—that he believed the Union men of the South to be in the majority in every seceded State, except perhaps South Carolina. If this is the truth, or any thing near the truth, as many signs prove that it is, then have we much to hope from the very quarter whence our trouble comes. At present, the Union sentiment of the South finds itself in the midst of a reign of terror, and is held in silence, as it were, by a military despotism. But give it an opportunity to speak and make itself felt, with assurance of protection and

aid from our national government, and treason, it is believed, would cower away out of sight, rebellion would throw down its arms, and a power would rise up to restore peace and order throughout the seceding States; would place the government of those States in loyal hands, and bring them back, happy to be restored to their place in the Union.

5. We have much to hope from the great moral forces which are on our side. The plan of God is always progressive. The wheels of his providence always move forward, and never backward. We live in the nineteenth century of the Christian era, and the forces to which I refer have, during that long period, been gradually but surely developing themselves, gaining strength and extending their influence in the world. Do you ask what these forces are? They are science, literature, religion, and civilization taken in its broadest christian sense. Now to what do these forces tend? On what great interests do they most directly bear? Is there one of them that acts in favor of the position taken by the South; that of establishing a confederacy and building up an aristocratical government based on slavery as its corner-stone, and for the purpose of extending and perpetuating the domain of slavery? Are the science, the literature, the religion, the civilization of our day in favor of a plan like this? Are they not rather directly opposed to it, branding slavery as a relic of barbarism and uttterly inconsistent with free institutions and all true progress of society? This appears to me just as certain as any problem in mathematics, and a government based on slavery, or in any way dependent upon it, or aiming to extend and perpetuate it as a leading object of its policy, has an element of rottenness in its very heart, and must sooner or later fall into decay and ruin.

But look at the forces I have referred to, in their bearing

on the cause we are engaged to support; and how plain is it that their combined influence is in favor of that cause; science in favor of it, literature in favor of it, religion in favor of it, all true civilization in favor of it! That cause, what is it? It is the cause of freedom, freedom of speech, freedom of the press, freedom of the elective franchise, the diffusion of general education, the support of free institutions and of true republican government. This is the cause, so comprehensive and so various, which the South, by its rebellion, is bringing into peril, and we of the North have risen up to defend. And shall we fail in what we have undertaken? Is there not hope, strong hope of success; seeing all the great forces now at work in advancing society and hastening on the great plan of God to its final consummation, are throwing their combined influence in our favor, and working for our victory? That victory may not be to-day nor to-morrow; it may even be *long* delayed, nor come without much cost of blood and treasure in contending with our maddened foe; but come it will, as sure as truth and righteousness and knowledge and civilization and freedom shall prevail over ignorance, barbarism, tyranny and crime. We can wait for the issue, if need be, wait in patience, good courage and hope, seeing we are moving on in the line of causes fixed as the throne of God, and sure of triumph as his own eternal kingdom of truth and righteousness.

6. We have much to hope from our past history. God has often appeared for us in times past, and delivered us from great and threatening evils. And we may be sure that he did not preserve this land of ours till so late a period in the world's history, and then plant here the tree of liberty, of knowledge and religion, finally to be overrun with despotism, with slavery, with ignorance and barbarism. No; the tree he planted here, he will defend; the institutions

established here by our pious forefathers under his fostering care, will be preserved; and the constitution and government which were secured for us by the great and good men who fought the battles of the revolution, and which have blessed this land, as no other land ever was blessed, for more than three-fourths of a century, will continue, we may confidently hope, to bless those who are to live after us, for long generations to come.

7. We may hope that the conflict in which we are engaged will not be long. This seems to be the opinion of those who have the best means to judge. And we may better adopt it than the opposite. It can not be, that so insane a war and for so insane an object shall last year after year, spreading its horrors and its carnage over this fair land. The madness of the hour will, I trust, ere long spend itself, and wiser counsels prevail. But whether the contest be long or short, let it be fought through, till an honorable peace can be had, based on principles of right, not soon to be shaken again. Let there be no peace by separation; that is impossible without the utter overthrow of our government and plunging the whole country into a state of anarchy, perpetual strife and war. And let there be no peace by compromise, by concession, by yielding to the unreasonable demands of the South; but peace when they have laid down their arms; peace *on and under the constitution*, peace on the great and only sure principles of peace, righteousness, truth and equal protection to the persons and rights of all. Then, out of the conflict, and as a consequence of it, we may hope that our institutions and government will come forth stronger, healthier, better and more established than ever. This I anticipate will be one result of the war. We shall have a stronger and more efficient government, and administered more according to the principles of justice, equity and right.

8. Finally, we may hope, as another result of this war, that slavery will receive its death blow, and at no distant day, disappear from our land. How this is to be done, I do not pretend to know. The overthrow of slavery was not, as I have before said, the original object of the war; nor is it now its proposed or avowed object. Nor should I desire to have this object held forth now as a thing directly to be aimed at. This it seems to me would be unwise and impolitic in the present state of the controversy, would create division among those who are now united in defending the Union, and tend to complicate the whole subject of emancipation in new and insuperable difficulties. Still I have a strong conviction, and certainly a most earnest hope, that emancipation will come as a consequence of this war. I do not exactly know how; God has the whole matter in his hands, and he, I think I see plainly, is in his wise and good providence, setting *various causes* in motion which will in the end, we may be sure, and at no distant day, root out slavery from our land, break every yoke and let every one held in bondage go free. I fully believe with Count de Gasparin, an eminent French author and statesman, who has recently published a most interesting volume on the present state of our country,—I fully believe with him, that the abolition of slavery will be one principal conquest of the nineteenth century. So may it be. And I will just add that the course pursued by the South, within the last few months, in exciting and carrying on this miserable rebellion, has done more to hasten the end of slavery, her nursling and her pride, than has been done by all the agitation and denunciatory counsels of ultra abolitionists for many years.

I here close what I have to say, though much more might be said, as to what we have to hope, and hasten to add a few words in regard to what we have to fear. After what has been said, you will readily infer, that I see no serious cause for apprehension. True, we see not the future, and know not what course affairs may take in our country. The phrase, *chances* of *war*, is full of meaning. The race is not always to the swift nor the battle to the strong. It sometimes happens in national conflicts, that the best cause suffers defeat and the strongest arm fails of victory. It may be so for a time with us. But if true to ourselves, there can be no reasonable ground of doubt that we shall come out of this war triumphant and our country be saved from dismemberment, established on a firmer foundation than ever.

Many have had fears lest Great Britain or France, especially Great Britain, might interfere to aid the South by weakening the blockade and otherwise affording her support. But whatever causes there may have been for apprehensions of this kind, they seem very much to have passed away. England will not enter into this quarrel; centainly not at present. It may be admitted that the nobility, the aristocracy of the kingdom, entertain no cordial love for us, or our form of government. They would willingly, at least many of their ruling ones, see our power broken, our growth checked, and our Union dashed on the rocks. The South have counted much on this, and have hoped long before this to be recognized as an established government, and to be received into relations of amity, and of trade and commerce. But hitherto she has been disappointed; she has gotten no countenance in her rebellion, and no encouragement from either France or England. And so it will be, we may hope, in the future. Whatever may be said of a portion of the English community, the great mass of the people, there can be no doubt, are true in their feelings of friendship towards us, and the motives must be very much stronger than they now are, before the rulers of the people will run so great a risk as that of provoking a war with us by interfering to afford aid and comfort to the South in its present posture of rebellion.

Our greatest cause of fear is, probably, the danger of becoming divided among ourselves. At present we are to a great extent united. The feeling is very general, and the determination is very firm, that the government must be maintained, and the rebellion must be put down at all hazards. This is as it should be, and God grant that both the feeling and the determination may continue in unabated strength and constant increase, till the consummation so devoutly to be desired, be fully attained. But should the war be prolonged and the taxes become heavy, and disasters multiply, as possibly they may, it would not be strange if the cry peace, peace, which we now occasionally hear, whispering from hidden conclaves and secret retreats, should wax louder and become more bold and urgent, till at length a party should rise up sufficiently strong to make itself felt; and then the demand would be, let us have peace, peace at any rate, even by submission to the South, acceding to her demands, and giving her the sceptre, if need be, to rule over us. This is our danger. Here lies our principal ground of fear. And yet I do not anticipate any great trouble from this quarter. I can not believe that the number will ever become large or formidable of such as would be willing to ask peace from the South while in armed rebellion against our government, or on conditions that would prostrate our free institutions and aid her in building up an empire whose foundations rest on slavery, as Vice President Stephens says, as its chief corner stone. I would commend to such, if any such are present, and to all others like them, throughout the land, could my voice reach them, the words of Mr. Douglas in his last speech, before referred to,—"Whoever is not prepared to sacrifice party organizations and platforms on the altar of his country, does not deserve the support of honest people."

I conclude with the remark that the greatest fear of all is, that we shall not, as a people, feel, in any measure as we ought, our dependence on God; shall not truly repent of our sins against him, nor seek his favor with that sincere humility and earnestness in prayer which are necessary to obtain his interposition in our behalf to deliver us from the evils we already feel, and avert from us the still greater which threaten to come upon us. This points us to the duty to which we are specially called to-day. And surely there is just cause for it. We are a sinful people; a people laden with iniquity; guilty before God, I am ready to think, beyond any other people on earth, and that because we have sinned against greater light and have abused greater privileges. On the score of justice we have nothing to hope, but every thing to fear from the almighty and righteous Ruler of the world. And whether the present is not the beginning of judgments which shall consume the land, until the people shall know and acknowledge that there is a God who ruleth in the earth, is a question which only he can determine. Our duty is plain. It is to search and try our ways; to humble ourselves before God for our individual personal sins, and the sins of our nation; penitently to implore his mercy to pardon, and his grace to interpose and save us. God alone is able to bring the deliverance we need in this time of our country's peril. His favor is absolutely essential to carry us through the terrible conflict which is now raging in our land, and restore peace and harmony to our distracted and suffering nation.

To him, then, let us go with all humility and godly sorrow, and offer to him such fervent, believing supplication, both for ourselves and our dear country, as will come up with acceptance before the throne of the great Ruler and Judge of the world, and engage him to remember us and his ancient mercy to our fathers, and turn again and save us. It is in this way only that we can perform aright the duties of this occasion, or be prepared to meet, in any proper manner, the unfoldings of that dark, mysterious drama that is now being acted in our country.

www.ingramcontent.com/pod-product-compliance
Lightning Source LLC
LaVergne TN
LVHW020742120826
845150LV00010B/2360

* 9 7 8 1 4 1 8 1 9 3 9 6 6 *